BORN IN A SECOND LANGUAGE

BORN IN A SECOND LANGUAGE

poems by

Akosua Zimba Afiriyie-Hwedie

Published by Button Poetry / Exploding Pinecone Press
Minneapolis, MN 55403 | http://www.buttonpoetry.com

Contents

BORN IN A SECOND LANGUAGE

or those for whom this need not be translated

ny grandmother does not know her hands are burning / she meets the heat in the grit
f its mouth / cooks / barehanded / ungloved / in English / says to me *it's hot* /
n Nyanja / says to me *it's too hot for you*

am three languages short of knowing myself / i only know one language well enough to
niss you in it / in elementary school / we are punished for language other than English /
n English / mother tongue smalls to tourist fodder / placed on third world shelf / not
or good dishes / English meant correct / mother tongue meant need for correction / in
English / i type / name my languages / am red lined into error / in English / names
ranspose / from kings and queens / Kgosi   Ohemaa / to Marys   Pauls / servants

n English / i know not to search for my name in your mouth / in Nyanja / i come up
hort / in Nyanja / i get lost / in Nyanja / my voice loses itself down my throat / in
Nyanja / i ask   *what does this mean in English?* / in English / i think i know what it means
 can pretend i do

ny parents met in English / a language learned / alongside each of their mother tongues
 this to say i was born / in a second language / born because of English

n English / i have voice but no culture / in Nyanja / my ears say to my feet /
ow come this body does not recognize its own tongue?*

1

Brenda Fassie wakes the dead

I soak in Brenda punching *Black President* through her lips like she wants this song to carry rocks in its hands just in case. I stand as my older brother sits beside me so I feel tall. & the last of a dead rain breaks against faint starts of a sun that should have switched off by now. *Weekend Special*, Brenda switches. I am too young, but this is the song the day needs. She kissed a girl, in print, in 1993 in South Africa. She made her life a song by allowing love into it. Maybe she thought that a lullaby sung into the hell of apartheid could switch off that fire. I slept and woke up in sweat from a nightmare; my brother's hand was there to answer. A girl's hand in another girl's hand sounds like an answer too. Brenda's fists sang like black coal like *too late   too late*—the only way left is to fight. I crossed the ocean to another man's country and left Brenda alone to fight. What I would give to hear her sing: *Nomakanjani . . . We dali wami* (No matter what . . . O my darling)   *Ungowami* (you are mine). This was the music before I left, before I became a sore in my lover's bed and forgot all I promised. What will I do with a love covered in lesions in a foreign man's country? I sit the songs behind my ears hoping to forget them. Between the insects and the names of the authors on the books, there is something dead in every corner of my room. *No, no, no*, she sings—play my song, *Ag Shame Lovely*, you cannot begin by breaking.

In my version

of the sky
flakes of gold
scatter. Most times,
I look beyond
God, pick one,
wish upon it.

Other times, I
look beyond God
for a woman
like my mother.

*

I cannot tell the woman
from the wound.
Both are so concerned
with your safety
they sit with you
until you heal.
And bleed and bleed and bleed.

Port of Entry

Welcome to the United States.

This form must be completed by all persons except U.S. Citizens.

When all items are completed,

this information may deny you entry to the United States.

Warning: Type or print legibly. Use English.

Failure to do so may delay your entry into the U.S.

You must surrender:

First (Given) Name

Family Name

Country of Citizenship

A nonimmigrant disposition is a violation of the law prior to surrendering.

You must surrender. Failure to do so may result in your removal.

Primary Inspection – Reason Referred:

U.S. Customs and Border Protection is not required to respond to this information

Secondary Inspection – Reason Referred:

U.S. Customs and Border Protection is not required to respond to this information

– –

SECTION III — DEPARTURE RECORD

i sit next to my body   between my body and its shadow

in America .   a country on its side

like a smoking baby   rocking beneath her mother's lit cigarette

i am a non-citizen   in a country   with its bootstrap down my throat

don't call this home   is written in my passport as a visa expiry date

don't call this home is afraid to be questioned   in a back room at immigration

don't call this home reminds me   while I am here   I need

to train myself constantly   to make room to leave

\<Please press here\>

Welcome   to   the   United   States

\<Generating\>

W e l c o m e t o t   h e U n I t e d S t a   t e s

          o m e   o   h   n   no home

          c o m   o   h   mooch
          c   m   o   h   S   Schmo
W e l   o m e   o   h   U n   s UnWholesome
W e l c o m e   U n   UnWelcome
          l c o   n I   S   t
          c   h e   a   ache

I know a place where I can spread myself out and be enough to fill a room

That place you said I'll find one day. Whose sky smells like Harlem. 116th & Lenox. Where Ghana found its way into America and waits for me in the market, on a table with beads. Where my hands are not my hands but my mother's. How lucky I'd feel, prepared. I'd hear the sun against my window. Pulsing its wanting eyes through the glass. And it will say, *Take and eat, this is my body.* I'd place my chin on the windowsill. And would take. And would eat. And my skin would grow even blacker from the joy of light. And God would see and know He sees a good thing. And He would say, *Let there be darkness.* And so darkness would not mean forsaken. And He would not say to separate it from light.

Remember what you told me? How I'd turn to my reflection in the glass, and my mother would be a proud face sounding out of me. Her hands looking into my body, seeing what a good thing I have become. I'd turn and America would be a man in the distance asking for forgiveness. Meaning it. And the woman wailing would not be my grandmother. And the woman wailing would not be me. And the woman wailing would not be 50 women in the living room at my grandfather's funeral, expected to perform their wailing every time a man walks in.

Eli, Eli, lama sabachthani?

How can I trust God
in the language   in which
He first forsook me   from 1619 through Îles des Chiens

to Cape Agulhas. How can I   when English makes a sentence
sink, iron gags and fastens mouths?

> *Dear God, so may it concern:*
> *if you will it,*
> *turn the wine back to water and replace these seas.*
> *Let me begin again*
> *with what is clean and will cleanse me.*

What my hands have learned

Afternoons were made of homework, English questions that needed English
answers, children running their playground-play grey knees beyond
the triangle patterned wire fences that lined each yard. Broadhurst
could not exist without trace of a ball knocking or a play-scream charting
an *out* or a *turn*. Every skin was black-shined with Vaseline.

When first asked, *Where are you from?* I was hardly old enough to hold my sentences
together, barely graduated from my mother's back. I thought
to open my mouth and let my English tell the asking boy each country one
by one:

Zambia, then Ghana, then Botswana. As if somehow my open
mouth and this day's English could unscramble Africa
and rejoin what was cut. But instead, I answered
first with my left hand, by grabbing the edge
of my brother's shirt, as if the stability of one hand prepared the task
for the other. Then with my right, by pointing to the house at the end
of that Broadhurst cul-de-sac, looking for my mother at the window
with kitchen water dripping from her hands.

Birthwrite // Mantswe

I was born after wrestling
with my mother for
hours. I was born eager
to tear something apart,
starting with her.
I was born upside
down and stayed.
On a dirt road,
I was muddy-mouthed
and sapping-born,
blackaching lyric, I
born Okavango Delta, thin
water hoarding
prayers. Rearranging body
parts I was born, shredding
my mouth off, dragging it
through dirt and replacing it,
replacing it with stones.

I beg Botswana back

down my throat
again
and
again.

I say *come*
                    into the belly,
                                into the womb
where we can recognize each other.

                                        Before my first words,
                                            I had your eyes.

Come back to me;
I cannot love
from outside my skin.

                I am a narcissist.
                            I only know to love what stays with me.

            I whispered my hand against your border,
            pushed you away,
            saying
                it's better to sever the neck on my own terms.

How did I mark myself as a victim in this story?—the same way a child pulls a
house from the paint, distorted. I forget I designed our separation.

conditioned

unkempt with childhood awe,
i sit in the room's middle
under comb and evening
in my half-done hair.
Brenda Fassie sings another Brenda Fassie
song from 1996, as my brother unbraids
my hair, the way my mother taught him to,
the way my father unbraids hers.

on the wall behind us, a boy's hands motion
as if curating, knitting a girl's head. each
loosened braid unravels to the floor.
at his hands, the girl's head gets smaller,
smaller and smaller.

I am deciding which language to spend the night in

I don't want to choose a mouth tonight.

Siniza yendesa. I won't rush.

      Undress first in Nyanja.

Brush

       with English.

Rinse

      in Nyanja. And repeat, again.

Make my bed with English. Spread

     the sheets in Nyanja. Wear my mother's shirt

          again. I cannot leave her

without taking something.

     I break the Nyanja words my mother gives me.

Keep to myself what I take from her.

Siniza yendesa. I won't rush.

     I won't slip on all I know and misname everything.

Say grace

A girl swallows her hands during supper.
She did not say grace and that was it:
Some learn more from what is removed from them.

She gave up milk and steak. Instead,
fed on the machine, hoping to come across a silver spoon.
Ate the cogs and flushed them down with grease.

Started to crack soot:
side effects on the way to glory.
She grew switchblade lips and broke

anything she spoke to for too long.
She cracked and cracked with no one to turn to:
Without begging hands, most Gods don't make time.

To-do list:

1. ~~Scrape nshima from my fingers to make room for more hunger~~
2. ~~Research ways to stop a running mouth~~
3. Ask my name if I've made home enough for it
   Unleash it,
   and see if it returns

4. ~~Mark the past hours that are safe to revisit, that give back joy when pressed~~

5. Serve my words before they expire

6. Say it: *I'm becoming an open window, a loosening belt*

Setswana lesson

Le kae? means *how are you?*

Also translates to *where are you?*

Response:

I am here   *Ke teng*

        Home is there
               wrapped in ambuya's chitenge
That way
            there
on our mothers' backs
            Home is Vaseline spread
          too thick on skin
                   like grease packed-in
                   hair barely long enough to bow
Home is braided   bowed and beaded

That way
           there
Home is what I know
          what I am

       I am here
            translating home
            a word at a time

                 home is far

Home is often explained by distance
because distant things in view are smaller
supposed to make home
easier to pick up and carry
                    put down and leave
I am here,
Ke teng means *I am here*

        but in answer to the greeting translates to
                I am fine—That is a lie   That is a lie

Long distance

Over the phone, my aunt says:
Since I'm in America, too,
I thought I should call to see how you are doing.
She's in Boston now though she lives in Zambia.
She never calls. But being in America seems to make the difference.
Only two days in America seems to make a difference.
I wonder why being in America does this.
I wonder what being in America has done for us. I wonder,
   what has being in America done for us? I wonder
   what has   *America done for us?* I wonder

   what has   *America done?*

   what   *for?*

      America *for us?* I wonder
   what   *America* *for us?* I wonder
   what   *in America* *for us?*

If I play Brenda Fassie now,

America might sound more like a church, like something I can dance in, like somewhere God can be found. Not 7 a.m. streets distressed about private business. Not the brown bark silence of my skin so loud in everyone's eyes it might as well be shouting. The point is, I have only my naked body and its hair wherever it grows. And Brenda, you're a dead woman I've been holding onto since you were alive. As if it's not already hard enough to be a woman, convincing the world that your body is yours, like your name is. Without someone like me holding onto parts of you as if you were mine. How long have I kept you Brenda? What is said now? *Sorry* or *I knew better, I just couldn't help myself.* Or *I saw you and thought you were mine to have.* I know these answers are on the money, or close to a man's word, or freedom. It's all the same, right? I was up late last night trying to make sense of the world. I started with Mars. And thought I'd gotten somewhere until I realized I was on the wrong planet. So far away that everything started to make sense. I had my body, my own moons, red lipstick. And roses that wouldn't get caught in my hair—the fake kind that never die or were always dead.

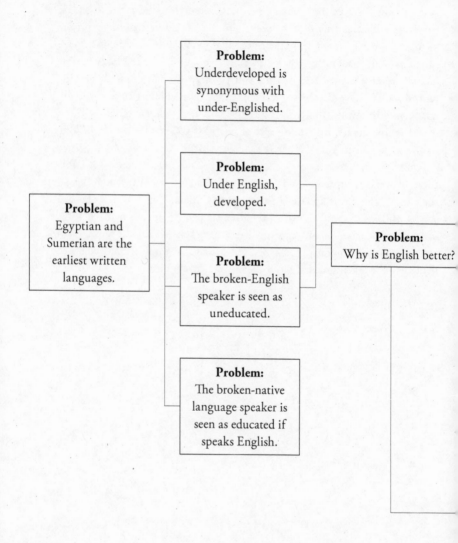

Problem:
What makes for better English?

Problem:
"Good" English examples: British English, American English . . .
"Bad" English examples: African American Vernacular English, Pidgin English . . .

Problem:
"Good" English sees colour. Certain colours have universal wealth; therefore, "Good" English has universal wealth.

Answer:
Whereas all languages are equal, some are more equal than others. Whereas English is Standard. Whereas not all English is acceptable standard. Whereas "good" English is more acceptable than others.

How to rebuild me when I fall apart

I want a spine
lined with cement,
a gun-barrel throat. A voice with steel boots.
An inside-out-turned tongue so the words come out right.

I want to command a lover who leaves me whole,
devours me. Wrings me out like wet clothes.

I want to rent my body to a soul brave
enough to carry it naked in the street. I want
to be naked in this body in the street.
To spoil the sky.

I want to beg the bottle, never to return
the alcoholic to the world without his drunkenness. I cannot tap moonshine
from between my legs and judge the drunk still.

I want only to hear the music
the instrument wants to play. I want a violin that pulls
its own strings,
a cymbal that hides its notes.

I want to be a man. Both poison and medicine.
choose to mix them up. Pour for my lovers
without heaviness when the body next to mine is cold.

To know the distinction between the two and still
at my leisure. Sleep easy at night. Wake up

I want what I deserve. Not just the shell

with the sound of the ocean but the ocean too.

I want to grow my own garden in my hair. I'm tired
refuse to navigate the nap and
I will not make the way straight and easy to follow for your sake.

of the flowers you give me. The ones that
knots in my path. I want to say *no*,

I want to play God. To give my breasts to the wailing cities. They would build an altar at my feet, give me
their last when their children are dying. I'd offer my dry breast, raw nipple. And when their mouths come loose, still
hungry, question their faith and never myself.

Akan Naming Chart, Day 1

In the Akan tradition, children are given first names according to the day of the week on which they are born.

Wɔfrɛ wo sɛn?

Akosua / Kwasi
(Sunday Born)

— named / for each virgin carrying oil / likewise for five talents doubled / the grace of lilac at the feather's hem / of a white-throated blue swallow / the swallow / for sage and the luxury of sense / the split second of fluorescent light in a passing alley / for simple math: one's word given and kept / *the good and faithful* / for blessings / the air's first breath after the church bell rings

For those of you who are home, welcome

Here, with marula trees and neighbourhood
tuck-shops, and grandmothers
like my grandmother
whose waists change colour daily
between chitenge. Pata patas
wet with rain-
smell soil. The most gorgeous rains.
Wouldn't these be the most gorgeous rains
if rains were known for being gorgeous?
Below the thin line of the equator
and above, lush and prayer-answered
rains. Summers alight with braais. And streets with names
like ours—Makeba, Nkrumah, Maathai, Kaunda. Brenda Fassie
and the music of our generation. Mtukudzi and our parents'
music. The music and what it does in us. I was born,
then watched the rest of this world happen. In the Botswana
of this world, past the Western bypass,
past the immigration building, past the next
traffic light, there is a house. On the third shelf
of the display case in the living room is a picture
of me in primary school uniform with pigtails
and a bunny-toothed smile that need
not do anything but keep smiling.

The incredible

at midnight:

1. my body is all wakefulness
    all moon in tight dress

2. my eyes hibiscus filled

3. a girl I do not know smiles at me

4. my body corrects itself

5. i smile back

6. my body corrects my chin
    growing above my back, consumed
    in the past

7. a man on the street and his silence pass me by

8. the shame i learned from Eve is Old Testament
    i am not church on broken knee

9. what is mine is mine, is mine alone

10. safely, i make it home

Outdooring Ceremony

If the ocean is always ahead of itself,
did it foresee its naming?
Did it foresee how it would become what it was called?

Provenance

My great great grandfather's head
looks nothing like my great great grandfather.
It's placed on its side in the Wallace exhibit,
in a museum in London. Oval-eyed, life
sized golden face with a cracked-open skull.

The description reads: *IT PROBABLY DEPICTS A DEFEATED ENEMY FROM A DIFFERENT ETHNIC GROUP.*

Not *probably*. I know this head.
My family's head. Ghana-gold the same
as the ring my father gave me with the signs
of the two angels he says watch over me.

The description reads: *THE HEAD WAS TAKEN BY BRITISH FORCES DURING THE ANGLO-ASANTE WAR.*

What is the utility of a detached head,
if the utility of a head is determined
by what it is connected to?

A sign reads: *THE MUSEUM IS NOT RESPONSIBLE FOR PERSONAL PROPERTY STOLEN OR FOR INJURY TO PERSONS OR PERSONAL PROPERTY.*

Then who is responsible for my family's head?
For our headaches?

In Twi, to say I have a headache, we say, *me ti y3 me ya*
which literally means *my head is paining me,*
which means *I am suffering from my head,*
which means *the head is a source of grief,*
which means *my grief is the distance from Ghana to London,*
which means *when the head is moved, the headache grows.*

I look as much like my Zambian mother
as I do like my Ghanaian father. The trick is
which country you look at me from and for how long.
The trick is who angles your head. The trick is whether
you believe a man can grow his likeness inside a woman.

There are no pictures of my father as a boy,
just as there are no pictures of my great great grandfather.
My father is the boys he once was and the men that followed. I know
my great great grandfather's face through my own and the man in it.
The men in my father's face show up in mine; I have their headaches.

How would your hands treat you if they were not yours?

As one man's flat palm violent against another's plain cheek, or as a fist softening-open to womb seeds into soil?

Have they taught you what to put together or how to pick apart?

Can the lines in your palm take you home?

*

A girl breaks down because she comes from a woman who is beside herself   because she has nothing to give besides herself.   The woman looks at the girl and opens her hands.   The woman hands the girl her hands   as if the girl does not already possess what belongs to her mother. Palm to palm.   They stare down, distress a sleeve running from each wrist.   Not knowing each palm   more than enough for the other.

Panacea

Fall asleep with the lights on to keep your enemies out.
The skies charting over you have no sense of falling.
A god in your mother's language will keep you alive.

When the universe and beings conspire
to make you think yourself
a moldy stain;
your voice, a damp spot,
spittle at the bottom of a glass:
say *one day at a time*, as your father used to.
Say what cat got your tongue,
then skin it,
skin it alive.

It goes without saying

My British English troubles my American English
I pause before I say words like *be-u-tea-ful*
Confused by how I learned to say it in Botswana,
In British English, and how I hear it here,
In America, there is less consideration for *u* in a sentence
How c o l o u r becomes c o l o r
Word flattened like somebody's version of this poor earth
And *We the people*
Is often *them* not *u, the people*
When I don't think in American English,
I think about *u* in almost every word, and it pains me
To know that *u* can't be in some places
That *u* should be
With me here in America, depending on who *u* are
Or who *u* aren't, the system is built to leave *u* out
If *u* go missing, the system isn't designed to miss *u*
I am always reminded that this is not my language
u can't be saved by any English
English was never meant to save *u*
Look at history, what English brought,
u didn't survive, so many of *u* didn't survive.

Life Cycle

Memory: There's the sound of the car lock
snap, smack shut like sucking teeth. An old me, child
strapped into the back seat of my mother's Nissan, whistling.
Whistling what?
I don't remember. God knows.
So does my mother.
So what woman couldn't do His job?

Now: I try to keep up with my body. My left hand cleaves to my right
breast under my shirt for want of something to un-idle. Each finger
spreads like a wide tooth comb, then one
around another, tangles.

If lucky, I won't have to be any more human
than I am right now.
I don't want to return in the next life
unless I'm an animal perched
in its own language.
A fiction, unalive
on paper, in 2D spun
from a child's pen.
Whatever is safe
from this life,
from what it cannot know.

Mama I've learnt a lesson

at the table early   in my Sunday best   a red suede dress two sizes too big
white frill beneath the buckle of my waxy black shoes   I hold my plate out for
gospel   but Brenda Fassie has prepared kwaito music   heat soaked in spit how
a mother chews food before she feeds her young   I cry   I want my music how I
want my music   I want gospel for Sunday the way the day meant it to be   but
Brenda says *the music makes the day   not the other way around*   she force
feeds me spoonfuls and spoonfuls   I want to cry again to spite her   but she's
right   my dry eyes eat and eat   watching her swirl the spoon as she songs
another plate   patterning waves of flower petals at the edges   like my mother
would serving porridge   like Brenda making for me a mother

Give us this day

I give this day to third-day rains, to sickness

in my body, to children with more time. I only

understand where things are from where I am

in the moment. Even my name was once

a strange thing I had to get used to. My religion

is coincidence, luck and God. I pray and I pray, not sure

to whom. Of course I love a boy who doesn't

like me. Of course I want to be wanted.

Of course about this, too, I prayed. I soak in a bath

of Epsom salt and my sins. For God so loved

the world that he gave and he gave. So his son

died in the giving. Show me on the world

where it doesn't hurt. Where it doesn't make

your faith tip and run dry. Before I could pray,

I used my first words to call my mother.

While Jesus wept for his father on the cross, I was held by mine.

Call me by my name

When God called the animals,
two by two. Each came

foreign unto itself. Only knowing its name once
told. A man is called into his name

each time it is spoken.
Or a man becomes more of himself

each time he is called by his name.
When my mother calls from a distant continent.

I must travel her voice to come into myself.
I measure how far I am from myself.

By the length it takes to walk along my mother's voice
into my name. When my mother sends for me

in my Twi name. I measure how far I am from myself.
By what language I use to respond. I learn

naming is how one becomes a self.
I know calling makes one return.

Notes

In "Akan Naming Chart, Day 1," the line "good and faithful" is a quote from Matthew 25:23: "Well done, good and faithful servant!"

"Birthwrite // Mantswe" is written after "i was born in a hotel" by Lucille Clifton.

In "Brenda Fassie Wakes the dead," the italicized lines *Black President*, *Weekend Special*, and *Ag Shame Lovely*, are titles of Brenda Fassie songs.

The following italicized lines are lyrics from Brenda Fassie songs:
too late too late is from the song "Too late for mama"
Nomakanjani . . . We dali wami is from the song "Nomakanjani"
No, no, no is from the song "No No No Señor"

"For those of you who are home, welcome" takes its title from the last line of a farewell announcement given by a flight attendant on a commercial airline.

"How to rebuild me when I fall apart" is written after "Romanticism (the Blue Keats)" by Roger Reeves. This poem was written at Callaloo and is dedicated to the brilliant Vievee Francis, whose teaching inspired the poem.

"Mama I've learnt a lesson" is a line from the song "Mama, I'm sorry" by Brenda Fassie.

"Panacea" is written after "The Conditional" by Ada Limón.

"Port of Entry" uses text found on form I-94 Arrival / Departure Record issued by United States Department of Homeland Security Customs and Border Protection.

In "Provenance" the lines *It probably depicts a defeated enemy from a different ethnic group* and *The head was taken by British forces during the Anglo-Asante war* are taken from an online description by the Wallace Collection Museum of the relic described in the poem.

Acknowledgements

I am grateful to the editors of the following journals and anthologies in which these poems, sometimes in different forms or with different titles, first appeared:

Bettering American Poetry Anthology: Reprint of "for those for whom this need not be translated"

Birdcoat Quarterly: "Akan Naming Chart, Day 1" and "Eli, Eli, lama sabach-thani?"

Kweli: "For those of you who are home, welcome"

Obsidian: "*Give us this day*" (Finalist of the 2020 Furious Flower Poetry prize)

Palette Poetry: "Provenance" (3rd place winner of the 2020 Emerging Poet's Prize)

PANK: "I know a place where I can spread myself out and be enough to fill a room," and "It goes without saying"

The Felt: "Brenda Fassie wakes the dead," "for those for whom this need not be translated" (as "i write for those for whom this will not need to be trans-lated"), and "I beg Botswana back"

The Napkin Poetry Review: "In my version"

TriQuarterly: "How to rebuild me when I fall apart"

Voicemail Poems: "Life Cycle"

Wildness Journal: "I am deciding which language to spend the night in"

Gratitude to my mum, dad, Yaw, grandparents & all my family; to Button Poetry without whom this chapbook would not exist; to the great Brenda Fassie whose music and boldness raised some of these poems; to HZWP for providing me time to write; and to my professors, especially Linda

Gregerson and A. Van Jordan; cohort and friends, especially David Wade, Erika Nestor, Pemi Aguda, Elinam Agbo, Augusta Funk, and Daniella Toosie-Watson; to my workshop instructors and cohorts at Callaloo, the Watering Hole and Cave Canem; to my teachers at Thornhill & Maru a Pula, especially Mrs. Brown; to Ilya Kaminsky and Marwa Helal for their generous and beautiful blurbs; to the good people who made this work possible in some way or another through friendship, and/or support, advice, feedback, encouragement, and kindness: Marwa Helal, Rachelle Parker, Marlin M. Jenkins, Akil Kumarasamy, Joshua Bennett, Morag Neill-Johnson, Naballah Hardy, Henry Lukoma, Comfort Tamanda Mthoto, Dolorence Okullo, Valentina Omoze Igenegbai, Clarisse Baleja Saidi, Carlina Duan, Christopher Greggs, K. Eltinaé, Joël Diaz, Johnette Marie Ellis, Nellie Scott, and Young Eun Yook; to all the journals that published my poems; to the many brilliant writers and artists who inspire me; to everyone who has been kind to and supportive of me and my work; to you and everyone who reads this little chapbook, thank you!

About the Author

Akosua Zimba Afiriyie-Hwedie is a Zambian-Ghanaian poet who grew up in Botswana. She holds an MFA in poetry from the University of Michigan. She placed 3rd in Palette Poetry's 2020 Emerging Poet Prize and is a winner of a 2019 Hopwood Award and a 2018 Meader Family Award. She is a finalist of the 2020 Narrative 12th Annual Poetry Prize, the 2020 Brunel International African Poetry Prize, the 2020 Palette Poetry Spotlight Award, the 2020 Furious Flower Poetry Prize, Wick Poetry Center's 2019 Poems for Peace and Conflict Transformation and received a 2020 Best of the Net nomination. She is a semi-finalist of the 2021 Great River Review Pink Poetry Prize. Akosua has received fellowships from the Helen Zell Writers' Program, Callaloo, and the Watering Hole. Her work has appeared or is forthcoming in *TriQuarterly, PANK, Kweli, Obsidian, Narrative,* and elsewhere.

AkosuaZah.com
Twitter: @akosuaZah

Other Books by Button Poetry

If you enjoyed this book, please consider checking out some
of our others, below. Readers like you allow us to keep
broadcasting and publishing. Thank you!

Neil Hilborn, *Our Numbered Days*
Hanif Abdurraqib, *The Crown Ain't Worth Much*
Sabrina Benaim, *Depression & Other Magic Tricks*
Rudy Francisco, *Helium*
Rachel Wiley, *Nothing Is Okay*
Neil Hilborn, *The Future*
Phil Kaye, *Date & Time*
Andrea Gibson, *Lord of the Butterflies*
Blythe Baird, *If My Body Could Speak*
Desireé Dallagiacomo, *SINK*
Dave Harris, *Patricide*
Michael Lee, *The Only Worlds We Know*
Raych Jackson, *Even the Saints Audition*
Brenna Twohy, *Swallowtail*
Porsha Olayiwola, *i shimmer sometimes, too*
Jared Singer, *Forgive Yourself These Tiny Acts of Self-Destruction*
Adam Falkner, *The Willies*
Kerrin McCadden, *Keep This To Yourself*
George Abraham, *Birthright*
Omar Holmon, *We Were All Someone Else Yesterday*
Rachel Wiley, *Fat Girl Finishing School*
Nava EtShalom, *Fortunately*
Bianca Phipps, *crown noble*
Rudy Francisco, *I'll Fly Away*
Natasha T. Miller, *Butcher*
Kevin Kantor, *Please Come Off-Book*
Ollie Schminkey, *Dead Dad Jokes*

Available at buttonpoetry.com/shop and more!